The Way of Walking Alone

Thank you very much for purchasing our book.
We would greatly appreciate it if you could take
a moment to leave us a review."

Dokkōdō

The Way Of Walking Alone

独行堂

Miyamoto Musashi

宮本武蔵者

We would like to thank you for your purchase by giving you an exciting gift.
You can DOWNLOAD FREE the first chapter of the book *The Life of Miyamoto Musashi* by entering on this link.
A amazing biography.

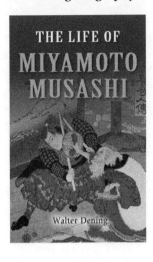

Dokkōdō, The Way of Walking Alone
Author: Miyamoto Musashi
Translation into English (from Spanish): Emily McPeek

© 2018 Shinden Ediciones, S. L.

www.shinden-ediciones.com
shinden@shinden-ediciones.com

First edition: September, 2018
Second edition: February, 2024

ISBN: 9798878564274

Design and composition: Shinden Ediciones, S.L.

CONTENTS

V

INTRODUCTION

Today, the original manuscript of the *Dokkōdō* is located in the Kumamoto Prefectural Museum of Art, to which it was donated after passing through different hands and in fulfillment of the wishes of its last owner: Takeshi Suzuki. This original was a part of the Toyota family patrimony since the times in which Toyota Masatake and his future descendants held the title of "War Advisers" of Yatsushiro Castle.

Both the twenty-one precepts that constitute the *Dokkōdō* as well as the *Go Rin No Sho* are dated seven days before the death of Musashi, and both of them address a single recipient, his disciple Terao Magonojō.

Scholars have compared the handwriting of the *Dokkōdō* with that of Musashi's existing letters, whose authorship is undoubted: for the former, what is conserved in the Eiji Yoshikawa Memorial Museum; and for the latter, what is deposited in the Yatsushiro Municipal Museum. The result is that the strokes, the pressure on the brush, the slant of the characters and, in short, the handwriting belong to the same person. Thus, there is no doubt that the *Dokkōdō* that is housed in Kumamoto was written by the hand of the great warrior Miyamoto Musashi.

LIFE OF MIYAMOTO MUSASHI

The details surrounding the childhood of Miyamoto Musashi are not clearly known, but it is believed that he may have been born in the year 1584 and, according to his own statement in his *Book of Five Rings*—*Go Rin No Sho* (五輪書)—, he was born in the province of Harima and his birth probably occurred in the village of Miyamoto, in the province of Mimasaka.

Miyamoto Musashi is known by various names: Shinmen Takezo (新免武蔵), Bennosuke—his childhood name—, Niten Dōraku—his Buddhist name—, Shinmen Musashi no Kami Fujiwara no Genshin—the name he used to sign his book *Go Rin No Sho* (五輪書)—and, lastly, Miyamoto Musashi (宮本武蔵), the name he has been generally known by. By using the name of the Fujiwaras in his book, Miyamoto Musashi wished to record that he was a descendant of this important lineage in Japan.

Musashi's father, Shinmen Munisai, was a consummated martial artist and an expert teacher in the handling of the sword and the *jutte* (十手), a sort of club with a fork that was often used by the police in that time. Munisai was the son of Hirata Shōgen, grandfather of Miyamoto Musashi and vassal of Shinmen Iga no Kami, lord of the castle of Takeyama

in the province of Mimasaka. One day, Lord Shinmen Iga
no Kami called for his vassal Hirata Shōgen and granted
him authorization to use the name Shinmen. This is why his
grandson Miyamoto Musashi would also make use of this
name later on.

In his youth and before then-*shogun* Ashikaga Yoshiaki,
Munisai was victorious in two of the three combats in which
he faced a renowned sword master named Yoshioka. It was
because of this prowess that the *shogun* himself granted him
the title of "Best in Japan". At that time, Munisai also dedicated himself to teaching *jutte* in his family's *dōjō*.

There is very little clear information, not just about the life
of Munisai—when and where he died, or even if he was really
the father of Musashi—but also about his mother.

With regard to Musashi's parents, there are diverse theories. The first claims that Munisai died in 1580, just as his
grave indicates, leaving behind two orphan daughters. This
contradicts what Musashi himself writes in *Go Rin No Sho*
about his date of birth. According to this theory, the late wife
of Munisai would later adopt a newborn baby boy from the
Akamatsu clan with the intention of turning him into the
successor of Munisai's *jutte* school, which implies that Omasa,
the widow of Munisai, would not have been little Musashi's
real mother.

The second theory proposes the idea that the date on Munisai's grave is incorrect and that, on the contrary, Munisai
enjoyed a long life, which would affirm that Musashi could

have been born to Munisai's first wife, Yoshiko. At the same time, it is possible that Munisai divorced his wife Yoshiko after the birth of Musashi, who remained under the tutelage of his father. Musashi would therefore have been raised in the care of Munisai's new and second wife, Omasa—daughter of Lord Shinmen of Iga.

Irrespective of all the theories that have been formulated about the ancestry of Musashi, what is clear is that, at age seven, he was educated by his uncle Dorinbo—or Dorin—in Shoreian Temple, three kilometers from Hirafuku. Both Dorin and his uncle-in-law educated Musashi in the values of Buddhism and basic intellectual skills such as reading and writing. Meanwhile, Munisai took charge of instructing Musashi in the handling of a sword and in the family art of the *jutte*. This period of instruction would not last long, because Lord Shinmen Sokan ordered Munisai to kill his own student, Honiden Gekinosuke, which forced Munisai to move far from the village of Kawakami.

Ultimately, the fate of his father is uncertain, but it is believed that he died at the hands of one of Musashi's future adversaries. In any case, there are no clear details about the life of Musashi or his family, being that the only written legacy he left us is related to the art of strategy and sword technique.

Miyamoto Musashi himself relates in his book *Go Rin No Sho* that he took part in his first fight to the death at the young age of thirteen. The unfortunate adversary was a warrior named Arima Kihei, trained in the heart of the Kashima

Shintō-ryū school, a style founded by the famous warrior Tsukahara Bokuden (1489-1571). Musashi also recounts how, when he was sixteen years old, he faced and defeated an adept swordsman named Akiyama, from the province of Tajima.

In 1599, Musashi left his town, apparently when he was barely fifteen years of age, and left all of his family possessions—including furniture, weapons and documents—to his sister and her husband, Hirao Yoemon.

In 1600, a civil war unfolded between the Toyotomi and Tokugawa clans. Musashi fought on the side of the Toyotomis, known as the "Army of the West", since the Shinmen clan—to whom Musashi's family owed a debt of loyalty—had allied with this clan. Musashi participated at the site of Fushimi Castle in July of 1600, in the defense of Gifu Castle the following month, and, finally, in the famous battle of Sekigahara in October of the same year, the battle which would decide the war in favor of the Tokugawa. However, as Musashi himself states in *Go Rin No Sho*, he would take part in six different battles.

As a result of the defeat of the Toyotomi army at Sekigahara, Musashi was forced to flee to Mount Hiko, and he was not heard from again until he was twenty years old when he arrived in Kyōtō, where it is well known that he entered into a series of duels not only against the Yoshioka school, but also against practitioners from numerous famous schools at that time—combats from which, according to him, he always emerged victorious.

As we have mentioned previously, Musashi's father had fought against a warrior of the Yoshioka school in his youth, receiving the title of "Best in Japan" as merit for his victory. The Yoshioka school descended from the Kyōhachi-ryū— "The Eight Schools of Kyōto". Legend has it that these eight schools were founded by eight monks who had been instructed by a legendary martial artist who inhabited the sacred Mount Kurama.

Musashi challenged Yoshioka Seijūrō, master of the Yoshioka school, who accepted the duel. Apparently, he faced Seijūrō's sword with nothing more than a *bokutō* (木刀)—a wooden sword. It is said that, after dealing him several forceful blows, he caused paralysis to Seijūrō's left arm. Because of this, control of the school passed into the hands of his brother, Yoshioka Denshichirō, who swiftly sought revenge on Musashi. The duel took place in Kyōto, near Sanjūsangen-dō temple. Musashi arrived late intentionally, and this made Denshichirō impatient and furious. Enough time passed that Denshichirō finally thought that Musashi had, out of fear, decided not to come; when he, now relaxed, went to leave, Musashi lunged at him and took him down quickly with a single blow to the head. This second victory constituted a grave offense for the Yoshioka clan, whose leadership then passed to a 12-year-old boy, Yoshioka Matashichiro. On this occasion, the Yoshiokas gathered a band of archers, gunmen and swordsmen, and then they challenged Musashi to a duel on the outskirts of Kyōto near Ichijōji temple. Unlike the previous duel, the intuitive Musashi arrived at the temple early and remained hidden until the Yoshiokas came. When they arrived, accompanied by all of their archers and soldiers, at just the right moment, Musashi jumped onto the young warrior Matashichiro, killed him and took off in a quick flight, clearing his path and fighting of every Yoshioka warrior who stood in his way. This duel led to the decline of the Yoshioka school.

After his stay in the city of Kyōtō, Musashi traveled to Nara, specifically to Kōfukuji temple, run by Buddhist monks who were experts in the *yari* (槍)—spear—of the Hōzōin ryū school. After fighting with the warrior monks, they allowed him to stay at the temple for some time, a period which he used to study their forms of fighting and their tradition of Zen Buddhism.

After leaving the temple, from 1605 to 1612 he traveled all over Japan as a *musha shugyō* (武者修行)—a warrior on a pilgrimage in which he limited himself to perfecting his skills through different duels. It is asserted that in all of these duels, Musashi only made use of his *bokutō*.

In 1607 while on his way to Edo, he faced, defeated and killed Shishido Baiken, a warrior who was an expert in handling the *kusarigama* (鎖鎌), a sickle with a chain and a weight on its end. One year later, in 1608, was the notorious duel between Musashi and Musō Gonnosuke, founder of Shintō Musō ryū. History tells us that these two great warriors fought on two occasions. In the first duel, Musō Gonnosuke faced Musashi armed with his *bō* (棒)—a 180 cm staff—being an expert in the handling of this weapon. After taking him down, Musashi, noting his adversary's proficiency and valor, let him go. This appears to be the reason why Musō Gonnosuke withdrew into the mountains in order to reflect on why he had been defeated. As a conclusion of all his meditation, his *jōjutsu* (杖術) system would later emerge, the art of fighting with the *jō* (杖)—a 126 cm staff. Musō Gonnosuke sought out his opponent and the two faced off in a duel once again, proving to Musashi that he was able to beat him with his new weapon.

In 1612, when Musashi was 30 years old, he participated in his most famous duel. It took place on the island of Ganryū, and his adversary was Sasaki Kojirō, who specialized in handling the *nodachi* (野太刀)—a saber that could measure more than 160 cm long. The duel was brief, and in it, Musashi killed his opponent with a wooden sword that he carved himself from the oar of the same boat that had brought him to the island. Being familiar with Sasaki Kojirō's use of the *nodachi*, Musashi designed his new weapon with the necessary length to stand up to his opponent's long sword.

From 1614 to 1615, Musashi took part in the war between the Toyotomis and the Tokugawas. This war broke out because Tokugawa Ieyasu considered the Toyotomi family to be an incipient threat to his government. In this contention, Musashi fought for the Toyotomi clan. Once again, he chose the losing side. The result of this war was the total defeat of Toyotomi Hideyori.

In 1615, he began working in the service of Lord Ogas-awara Tadanao of the province of Harima, carrying out the role of "construction supervisor". Thus, he collaborated on the construction of Akashi Castle and participated in the urban design of the city of Himeji at the end of 1621. During his time working for this lord, he also dedicated himself to teaching the martial arts, primarily the discipline of *shurikenjutsu* (手裏剣術)—techniques for throwing weapons. It was during this time that he adopted his first son, who in 1626, in accordance with the tradition of *junshi* (殉死), committed the act of ritual suicide—*seppuku* (切腹)—because of the death of his lord of Himeji, to whom he was a loyal vassal.

In 1627, Musashi resumed his travels and, in the early 1630s, he settled in Kokura, where he joined the service of the *daimyō* (大名) Ogasawara Tadazane and where he would later play a fundamental role in the Shimabara rebellion.

Afterward, in 1633, Musashi moved to the castle of *daimyō* Hosokawa Tadatoshi in Kumamoto. During this stage of his life, he participated in very few duels and conflicts. One of them took place in 1634, in which he defeated a spear expert named Takada Matabei. Musashi officially became a servant of the Hosokawa lords of Kumamoto in 1640.

In the year 1642, Musashi's health began to decline, and in 1643 he retired as a hermit to a cave known by the name of Reigandō, where he set himself to writing his most well-known work: *Go Rin No Sho*, which he finished in the second month of 1645. Being conscious of his imminent death, he decided to leave all of his possessions and a copy of the manuscript of *Go Rin No Sho* to his closest student, Terao Magonojō. It was seven days before his death when he wrote the twenty-one precepts of the *Dokkōdō*, which he, in turn, dedicated and transmitted to his disciple. Finally, he passed away in Reigandō on May 19, 1645.

Dokkōdō

独

行

堂

世々の道をそむく事なし

宮本武蔵

Do not rebel against
the paths of this world.

独行堂

身にたのしみをたくます

宮本武蔵

Do not seek out
physical pleasure.

独行堂

よろつに依怙の心なし

Do not place your
trust in anything.

身をあさく思世を

ふかく思ふ

宮本武蔵

Give less importance to yourself
and more to the world.

一生の間よくしん思わす

Avoid thinking in
a covetous way.

我事におゐて後悔をせす

Do not reproach yourself
for your past actions.

善悪に他をねたむ心なし

宮本武蔵

Do not be envious of the
good or the bad in others.

いづれの道にもわかれを
かなします

独行堂

Do not regret that
which has gone away.

自他共にうらミか

こつ心なし

Do not feel bitterness
towards yourself or others.

れんほの道思ひよる
こころなし

十

Do not let your spirit
be carried away by
romantic passions.

物毎にすきこのむ事なし

Do not be guided by
your preferences.

私宅におゐてのそむ心なし

独行堂

Do not desire to possess
a luxurious house.

身ひとつに美食をこのます

Do not seek pleasure
from food.

末々代物なる古き

道具所持せす

Do not possess valuable relics
to leave in an inheritance.

わが身にいたり物
いミする事なし

宮
本
武
蔵

Do not do things that may
physically harm you; it makes
no sense to do so.

兵具ハ格別よの道具
たしなます

Do not seek out sophistication
in your weapons as a warrior.

道におゐて八死を
いとわす思ふ

Do not fear the death that
may meet you on the Path.

老身に財寶所領
もちゆる心なし

Do not work with the intention
of possessing riches in old age.

佛神ハ貴し佛神をたのます

Respect the gods and the buddhas;
do not rely on them.

身を捨ても名利はすてす

Even on the brink of death,
never abandon your honor.

常に兵法の道をはなれす

宮
本
武
蔵

Never stray from the
Path of the Art of War.

正保貳年

　　五月十二日

　　新免武藏玄信

　　　　寺尾孫之丞殿

宮本武蔵

Year 2 of Shoho,
May 12,
Shinmen Takezo Genshin
For Terao Magonojō.

*This edition is dedicated to the memory of
all those warriors who, with their lives and
sacrifice, have preserved the martial arts traditions.*

The Editor.

Made in United States
Orlando, FL
03 October 2024

52296395R10040